North Carolina
Simply Beautiful

Photography by
Robb Helfrick

FARCOUNTRY
PRESS

In memory of Pat Conner and Ann Conner—
two spirited North Carolina women.

FRONT COVER: Picturesque Linville Falls drops into a deep gorge along the Blue Ridge Parkway.

FRONT FLAP: Hints of spring color in a forest near Albemarle.

BACK COVER: Pea Island National Wildlife Refuge stretches 12 miles along the Atlantic Coast from Rodanthe to Oregon Inlet.

TITLE PAGE: A sad little basset hound peeks through a fence.

RIGHT: Sunrise illuminates the sky over Bodie Island Lighthouse on Cape Hatteras National Seashore.

ISBN 1-56037-256-7
© 2003 Farcountry Press
Photographs © Robb Helfrick

Created, designed, and published in the USA. Printed in China.

North Carolina is a place that stirs the senses and awakens the spirit. This gracious southern state is defined not by random lines of longitude and latitude, but more by its welcoming people, fascinating history, and beautiful landscape. The state boundaries enclose a territory that stretches 503 miles from the ancient Appalachians to the shallow shoals of the Outer Banks. Travel along its backroads and highways reveals a place that has managed to hold onto the simple traditions of the past, without sacrificing the promise and progress of the future. From the highlands of the west through

itself, which has been hundreds of millions of years in the making. This is most evident to the eye in the Great Smoky Mountains. A breathtaking region of beauty and diversity, with rounded peaks and sheltered coves, the Appalachians are America's oldest mountain range. The view from the summit of Clingmans Dome, at an elevation of more than 6,000 feet, is one of overlapping mountain ridges that soften and melt into a distant horizon. In early summer, the hills are speckled with mountain laurel, flame azalea and catawba rhododendron; in autumn, the senses are overwhelmed with the dazzling display of red maple and sourwood trees. On a clear day, this vista also affords a glimpse of 6,684-foot-tall Mount Mitchell, the tallest peak east of the Mississippi River. This is the roof of North Carolina.

The lush forests and rocky streambeds of the Smokies shelter an amazing variety of plant and animal species. This ecosystem boasts more varieties of trees than found in all of Europe, and is home to more than one thousand different types of wildflowers. There is a pleasant collision of northern and southern species found here, so a trip up a steep mountainside can be almost like a visit to Canada. Exploration of the half-million-acre Great Smoky Mountains National Park also conjures up an image of the simple and challenging life that the pioneers faced in their mountain communities. The vestiges of this bygone era are preserved in places such as Cataloochee and Oconaluftee, with their rustic mills and old homesteads.

Traveling away from the Smokies, with all of North Carolina spread out before you, a drive on the Blue Ridge Parkway is the most picturesque way to head east. A trip from Soco Gap to Richland Balsam offers the opportunity to experience different seasons in a single day. As the road dips and turns and then gains elevation, it is possible to leave spring behind on an April day and enter back into the chill of winter at loftier points on the road. In more temperate months, you can gaze from one of the many parkway overlooks and see no signs of human development. A carpet of trees obscures all evidence of civilization, and the only thing visible on this undulating, colorful rug are distant peaks with names like Grandfather and Pisgah. When fog and mist creep in and cover the landscape, a common sight in these mountains, the mood changes, and the view is transformed into one of ghostly shapes and silent stillness. All this awaits the wide-eyed traveler on North Carolina's most scenic byway.

This downtown Charlotte monument commemorates America's first gold rush, which was sparked in 1799 when twelve-year-old Conrad Reed found a glittering nugget in a creek near his home in Cabarrus County.

the rolling hills of the Piedmont, to the wetlands along the coast, North Carolina carries itself with a gentle grace and a subtle grandeur. This wonderful character is a testament to the ideal synergy between man and nature, experienced throughout the year in the Tarheel State.

North Carolina earned its statehood in 1789, two hundred years after its first pioneers arrived in present-day Dare County. This interval of modern-day history is but a few seconds in geologic time when compared to the land

The Piedmont connects North Carolina's mountains to its celebrated seacoast. It is the cosmopolitan and geographic center of the state. This is where the majority of its citizens live and work. From the city of Charlotte, with its impressive skyline, strong banking industry, and rich cultural identity, to downtown Raleigh, where state government rules, North Carolina moves to a modern beat. In Greensboro and Winston-Salem, history mingles with commerce and comfortable living. Chapel Hill and Durham offer higher education and college basketball, each with impressive legacies. This is a region noted for its furniture craftsman-

ship—Highpoint is the epicenter—as well as being the location of America's first gold rush. Outside the cities, in a patchwork of small towns and rural areas, life is enjoyed and lived to its fullest. Business is conducted in county courthouses that are architectural gems, families gather in local parks, and farmers till the fields.

The foothills of the Piedmont fade away on a drive east from Charlotte. As the landscape rests and lies down horizontally and flat farm fields come into view, you have reached the birthplace of North Carolina. It is here, in this domain of small fishing villages, idle rivers, and colonial towns, that the state began its evolution. This is the Coastal Plain. Two interesting communities found here, Edenton and New Bern, recall the early days of the state's development. The seat of government moved westward to Raleigh long ago, yet they both retain their Old World charm and classic architecture. Wilmington is more of a bustling town, but it has retained its bountiful heritage too—it boasts the state's largest historic district and a restored waterfront. There are many other enchanting towns in this region, where tree-lined streets shelter plantation-era homes by the water's edge and quaint churches seem to stand on every corner.

There is a change in the character of the water when it reaches the Coastal Plain. Rivers that rushed all the way from their origin in the mountains meander here and take their lazy time reaching the sea. North Carolina is home to America's largest inland shoreline, so one could spend a lifetime exploring the tidal creeks, swamps, and sounds and never see it all. The tides and the seasons produce a natural rhythm here that is both peaceful and eternal. There is an abundance of wildlife throughout this area. Great blue herons and other wading birds fish in the shallow waters. Waterfowl

A storm stalks the coastal town of Edenton.

congregate in ponds and are silhouetted by the setting sun. There are several national wildlife refuges close to the coast, and they provide a safe habitat for many native and migrating creatures. Hidden from view, in two million acres of estuaries, are the next generation of shellfish. This coastal ecosystem is protected and preserved in part by a chain of barrier islands. This area of coastal North Carolina is famously known as the graveyard of the Atlantic: the Outer Banks.

The draw of the water and the lure of the coastline is palpable when one approaches the Outer Banks. Despite its fearsome reputation as the place where ships go to die (more than 2,000 vessels have been lost here since colonial days), an excitement can be felt for this land of shifting sand and massive dunes. Another world awaits—one with a storied past and an ever-changing beauty. Standing sentinel over the landscape are six lighthouses, each with its own distinct painted design and light flash sequence. Modern navigational tools have greatly diminished their significance to mariners, but they remain a treasured

legacy of American architectural history. Along with the lifesaving stations that operated here in the past, the lighthouses rescued many lost souls and gave comfort to those who traveled the treacherous waters of the Outer Banks.

There are sleek boats and brightly colored vacation homes scattered about in towns such as Nags Head and Avon, but the most impressive sights around the Outer Banks are not the creations or possessions of man. At Jockeys Ridge State Park, one can climb the East Coast's tallest sand dune and enjoy a panoramic view from the top. It's only natural to let your mind wander here and think of Orville and Wilbur Wright. One hundred years ago, in nearby Kitty Hawk, they utilized the soft sand dunes and the reliable winds to achieve man's first flight. Farther south, when crossing over Oregon Inlet, it is both awesome and terrifying to realize that a single Atlantic hurricane created this passage to the ocean. The constant interaction of wind, water, and sand creates an infinite number of forever-changing patterns and natural compositions along the shore. It is a wonderful place to relax and gain a healthy respect for the forces of nature.

North Carolina offers an infinite variety of experiences and sensations, and each one makes an imprint on the mind and is worthy of recollection. They may be simple gifts—fleeting at best—but they stay with you if you let them in. In North Carolina, these memories draw near with little effort, and they come often. There is magic in the quality of light found when the sun hangs low over the marsh, there is simplicity in the muffled sound and quiet stillness after a mountain snowfall, and there is contentment in the creak of a rocking chair on a comfortable front porch. These moments can be found anywhere, if you stop and search for them. In North Carolina, it's just a little easier: they find you.

ABOVE: A blaze of autumn color along Lake Toxaway Falls.

RIGHT: A mountain biker enjoys a choice single-track in Tsali Recreation Area.

FACING PAGE: Morning sunlight reflected on the Alligator River in the eastern part of the state.

ABOVE: The 18th-Century Backcountry Farm at Gastonia's Schiele Museum interprets life in the early days of North Carolina history.

LEFT: A rustic rail fence swaths a sea of buttercups in the far western corner of the state.

ABOVE: An intrepid surfer challenges the roiling surf at Wrightsville Beach.

FACING PAGE: Built in 1886, the Union County Courthouse in Monroe has been restored and is on the National Register of Historic Places. The building now holds county offices and a Heritage Room containing historical documents.

ABOVE: Eastern brown pelicans enjoy the docks and harbors of coastal North Carolina. These large birds were once on the endangered species list, but with the help of conservation efforts, they are now abundant on the southern coast.

LEFT: Lake Mattamuskeet is the largest natural lake in North Carolina; its average depth is only two feet.

ABOVE: Summer flowers bloom outside the
Lick Log Mill crafts store in Highlands.

RIGHT: Tulips announce spring in Fayetteville.

ABOVE: In beloved remembrance in Edenton.

FACING PAGE: As if in a dream, this Blue Ridge Parkway cabin recalls simpler days.

ABOVE: A closeup look at Mingo Falls, which drops down a rocky mountain-side in the Great Smoky Mountains near Cherokee.

RIGHT: The Greek-Revival-style North Carolina State Capitol was completed in 1840. The capitol's exterior walls are made of gneiss stones weighing as much as ten tons each.

ABOVE: The University of North Carolina at Chapel Hill's Memorial Hall is undergoing a major renovation project that will update and expand the auditorium's features.

LEFT: The rapids of the Oconaluftee River in Great Smoky Mountains National Park are popular with kayakers and whitewater rafters.

FOLLOWING PAGES: Dazzling autumn scene below Grandfather Mountain along the Blue Ridge Parkway.

ABOVE: Abandoned boat in a salt marsh near Sunset Beach.

LEFT: Cardinal finds shelter in the large leaves of a palmetto tree. The cardinal is North Carolina's state bird and a year-round resident.

FACING PAGE: Charlotte is North Carolina's largest city, and it continues to grow at a rapid pace.

All in a row at Oregon Inlet. Due to its prime position on the Outer Banks, Oregon Inlet has become a popular charter fishing destination.

ABOVE: Brightly colored homes welcome vacationers to Atlantic Beach.

RIGHT: Light fog softens the view in this Blue Ridge Parkway forest.

ABOVE: Rafters go over falls on the Nantahala River near Wesser.

LEFT: Fog can't hide the radiant red and yellow autumn leaves along the Blue Ridge Parkway.

ABOVE: An interior hallway at Fort Macon, a brick and stone five-sided fort built to protect North Carolina's coast from pirates. The fort was used extensively during the Civil War.

RIGHT: A street scene from the past at Old Salem living history village in Winston-Salem.

ABOVE: Old Locke Cotton Mill building in Concord.

LEFT: Almost every shade of green you can imagine graces this hillside near Devils Courthouse on the Blue Ridge Parkway.

ABOVE: Oconaluftee Indian Village in Cherokee celebrates two centuries of Cherokee Indian culture and tradition.

RIGHT: White-tailed deer are a common sight in the North Carolina mountains. In spring, a nourishing velvety cover grows over a buck's antlers.

ABOVE: Snow leopard at Soco Zoo in Maggie Valley.

LEFT: Spring buds announce a change of season outside Goldsboro City Hall.

ABOVE: Farm buildings at the Carl Sandburg Home in Flat Rock. This national historic site honors the literary figure and North Carolina resident for his work on behalf of people who could not speak or write for themselves.

RIGHT: Old wagon wears Christmas colors.

FACING PAGE: A bushel of apples ready for pressing at High Hampton.

Purple sunset over 6,643-foot Clingmans Dome. Though actually in Tennessee, this tall peak can be seen from many points in North Carolina.

ABOVE: A carefree evening swim on a lake near High Point.

RIGHT: The Blue Ridge Parkway curves through the mountains near Soco Gap.

FOLLOWING PAGES: A quintessential symbol of North Carolina: the Cape Hatteras Lighthouse on Cape Hatteras National Seashore.

ABOVE: A great egret's bright white plumage stands out in the greens and browns of this marshland along Alligator River.

LEFT: The North Carolina mountains have several good fly fishing streams.

FACING PAGE: Early morning scene along the Nantahala River.

ABOVE: You lookin' at me? Gray squirrels live throughout North Carolina.

RIGHT: The proud Cabarrus County Courthouse was built in 1876 out of handmade bricks.

FACING PAGE: Dogwood grows throughout North Carolina, from the mountains to the coast. It is the North Carolina state flower.

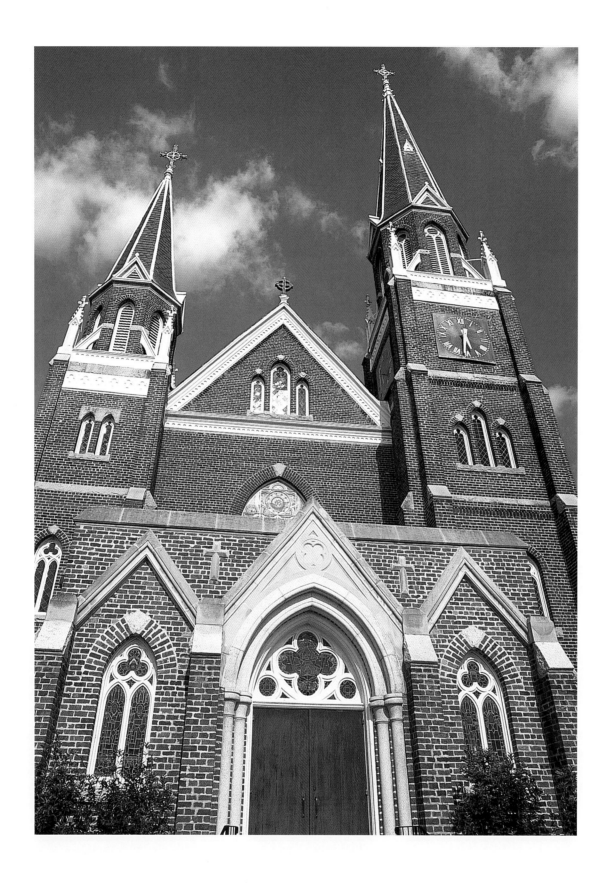

ABOVE: The Basilica of Mary Help of Christians on the campus of Belmont Abbey was partially constructed by the monks living at the monastery in the late 1800s. The church's painted glass windows were part of a display that won four gold medals at the Columbian Exhibition of 1892.

FACING PAGE: An architectural and historic treasure, the Bellamy Mansion in Wilmington, with its Corinthian columns, is a well-preserved example of antebellum construction.

ABOVE: Sitting on the verandah at Highlands Inn and Restaurant in Highlands.

RIGHT: Glorious Dry Falls near Highlands drops more than 75 feet. A paved trail leads to the falls from a nearby parking area.

ABOVE: Soft-shelled crabs for sale in Sunset Beach.

LEFT: Along the waterfront in Beaufort, a historically significant seaport and popular Atlantic Coast destination. This coastal town is nearly three hundred years old.

ABOVE: The brilliant stained glass windows of Duke University Chapel portray stories from the Old and New Testaments.

FACING PAGE: The Swanquarter National Wildlife Refuge offers sanctuary for black ducks, osprey, colonial waterbirds, and one of the northernmost populations of alligators.

ABOVE: A young pine flourishes even under its snowy burden.

LEFT: The secluded Honeymoon Cottage on Jewel Lake, part of the High Hampton Inn lodging complex.

ABOVE: A great blue heron struts along the North Carolina coast.

RIGHT: Ice patterns on a frozen lake near Andrews.

FACING PAGE: The *Elizabeth II*, usually moored at Manteo, is a replica of the ship that brought the first English-speaking settlers to North Carolina.

After a snowfall in the Great Smoky
Mountains near Maggie Valley.

ABOVE: Light blue skies and soft rays of sunshine promise spring will soon come to the Blue Ridge Parkway.

RIGHT: The Bell Tower of North Carolina State University in Raleigh chimes every hour.

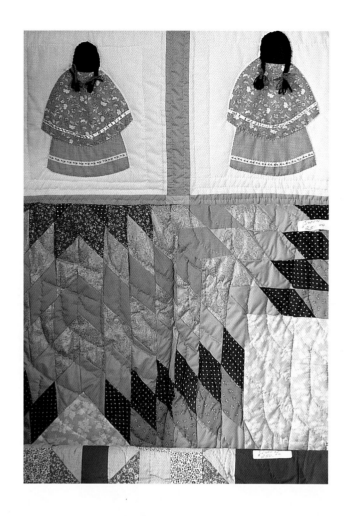

LEFT: Closeup of a handmade quilt in Cherokee, headquarters of the Cherokee Indian Reservation.

BELOW: The Mecklenburg County Courthouse in Charlotte houses the Law and Government Library and many judicial offices.

FACING PAGE: Cascades on Alum Creek in Great Smoky Mountains National Park.

ABOVE: Horses graze in a pasture near Hickory.

RIGHT: Built in the 1760s by Royal Governor William Tryon,
Tryon Palace served as North Carolina's first state capitol.

ABOVE: A Revolutionary War cannon at Guilford Courthouse National Military Park.

LEFT: The sun glows red over the North Carolina coast.

ABOVE: The Biltmore Estate in Asheville was conceived and financed by millionaire George Vanderbilt as a retreat for his family and friends. It is America's largest privately owned home and is now open to the public.

FACING PAGE: View from the top of Bald Head Island Lighthouse.

ABOVE: Though usually white, dogwood petals also come in bright pink.

LEFT: A sprinkling of pink, catawba rhododendron blooms along the Blue Ridge Parkway near Richland Balsam.

ABOVE: Bodie Island Lighthouse's stripes are 22 feet tall.

RIGHT: The sun is a natural spotlight warming these trees in the Great Smoky Mountains.

ABOVE: Fog is a common visitor to the Blue Ridge Parkway.

LEFT: Hand-carved duck decoys on Ocracoke Island. Decoy carving dates back to the days when anglers made a living hunting ducks in the off season.

FACING PAGE: Rocking chairs on the front porch of Richmond Hill Inn in Asheville.

Thunderstruck Ridge often leaves Blue Ridge Parkway tourists awestruck.

The 144-year-old Cape Lookout Lighthouse was purchased from the U.S. Coast Guard by the National Park Service in 2003. This landmark is at the southernmost point of Cape Lookout National Seashore.

ABOVE: Ready for the fishermen at a Davis marina.

FACING PAGE: A peaceful spring morning along the Blue Ridge Parkway.

ABOVE: Wild azalea along Newfound Gap Road in Great Smoky Mountains National Park.

FACING PAGE: The distinctly modern Charlotte skyline as seen from Marshall Park.

ABOVE: American coot negotiates the sandbars in a coastal marsh.

RIGHT: Morning light on a home in New Bern's historic district.
New Bern is the second oldest town in the state.

ABOVE: Wide-based Bald Head Island Lighthouse, built in 1817 and retired in 1935, is the oldest lighthouse in North Carolina.

LEFT: A forest in the making in Great Smoky Mountains National Park.

ABOVE: Eastern brown pelican lounges on a dock at Oregon Inlet.

RIGHT: This beautiful, quiet scene belies the fact that Oregon Inlet was formed by a severe 1846 hurricane that cut a new channel in the Outer Banks.

ABOVE: Sun and surf put on an early morning show at Indian Beach.

RIGHT: Wide-eyed but delicate bluets grow near Soco Gap.

FACING PAGE: Fresh snow and light fog glow purple in a Soco Gap forest at about 4,340 feet above sea level.

ABOVE: A basset hound snoozes on a rustic porch in the western mountains.

LEFT: Probably the oldest existing church in North Carolina, St. Thomas Episcopal Church in Bath was constructed of solid brick in 1734.

FOLLOWING PAGES: The classic rolling ridges of North Carolina's mountains.

ABOVE: Spring color frames the Old Gaston County Courthouse in Dallas.

FACING PAGE: Sculpted figures in Manteo's Elizabethan Gardens, a memorial to North Carolina's first English colonists.

ABOVE: Roses bloom at the historic 1804 Memorial Garden in the heart of Concord.

LEFT: A storybook scene along the Blue Ridge Parkway.

ABOVE: Home of the Carolina Panthers, Ericsson Stadium's exterior resembles a palace more than a football venue.

LEFT: Sunburst scatters fog on a Great Smokies ridge.

ABOVE: Stocked and ready at the old harbor in Southport.

FACING PAGE: Closeup of bright yellow crab traps on the coast.

ABOVE: A kayaker dauntlessly paddles through rapids on the Nantahala River.

LEFT: Looking up through red autumn leaves.

ABOVE: Dedicated in 1932, this granite monument atop Kill Devil Hill commemorates Wilbur and Orville Wright's first successful flight.

FACING PAGE: Shifting sand at Jockeys Ridge State Park in Nags Head.

ABOVE: Old Salem, a living history town, remembers the Moravians who settled in northern North Carolina in 1766.

LEFT: Fishing supplies on a Hog Island dock. Fishing remains an important North Carolina industry.

ABOVE: Befitting their color, yellow trillium flowers have a citrusy lemon scent.

RIGHT: Mingus Mill in Great Smoky Mountains National Park still operates, grinding corn using nineteenth-century equipment.

ABOVE: The restored Bost Grist Mill in Cabarrus County contains historic milling equipment and artifacts.

LEFT: A grassy dirt road beckons fall color enthusiasts.

FOLLOWING PAGE: Cape Hatteras Lighthouse will remain on duty during the night.

119